T0272837

Printed in the USA
CPSIA information can be obtained
at www.ICGtesting.com
JSHW062047291024
72532JS00017B/113

9 780874 413892

A Jewish prayer book is called a Siddur — סִדּוּר. Color this cover and write your name on the line. Can you write your name in Hebrew? Write it on the cover too. You can use this cover and the other pages in this book to make your own Siddur.

SIDDUR

סִדּוּר

_____
Name

שֵׁם

תְּפִלּוֹת are prayers. Many תְּפִלּוֹת are written in the Siddur. A young girl could not read the prayers in the סִדּוּר. But she did know the letters of the Hebrew alphabet. She prayed by repeating the letters of the alef bet over and over again. Then she asked God to make the letters into beautiful prayers. Can you help the girl to say her תְּפִלּוֹת? Find the letters that spell the Hebrew word for prayers. Cut them out and paste them on the spaces in the correct order.

The סִדוּר is a very important book. It contains prayers we say to God, and words that God sends to us. We take special care of a סִדוּר. We never let it touch the floor. We keep it clean and safe. God's name often looks like this in the siddur — יְיָ. When we pray we pronounce God's name "Adonai." Look closely at the picture and see how many times you can find God's name.

When you say nice things to someone, you praise that person. Our סִדוּר is filled with praises of יְיָ. Many of our prayers begin with the word בָּרוּךְ. It means blessed or praised. We praise יְיָ for many things. It is one way of saying "thank you" to God. Color the things you thank יְיָ for.

בָּרוּךְ
blessed

When we pray, we are talking to God. When we talk to God we say "You" — אַתָּה.
When we pray to God we say, "בָּרוּךְ אַתָּה יְיָ." It means, "Blessed are You, Adonai."
Take your prayer from בָּרוּךְ אַתָּה to יְיָ. There are different ways through the maze.
See how many ways you can find to take your prayers to God.

When we pray together, each one of our little prayers becomes one big prayer. When we pray together, we pray to OUR God. The Hebrew word for Our God is אֱלֹהֵינוּ. Help them join their prayers together by drawing them holding hands. Help them say their prayers by completing the Hebrew word for Our God.

מֶלֶךְ is the word we use to show that God is powerful in the world. מֶלֶךְ means ruler like a king or queen. It shows that God is in charge of the world. Connect the dots to see a picture that reminds us that יְיָ is King.

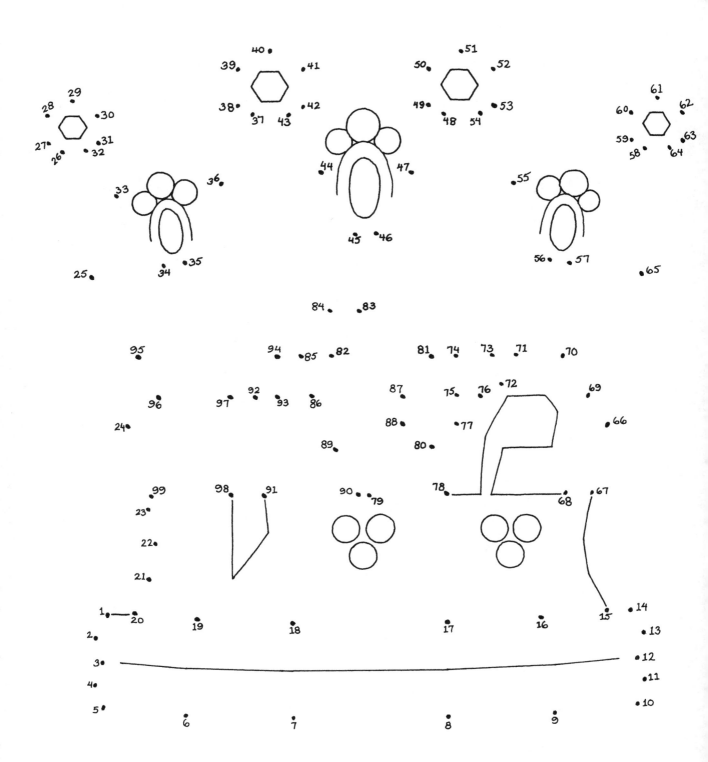

In our prayers we say that God is "ruler of the whole world." The Hebrew way to say "the world" is הָעוֹלָם. There are millions of people, animals and plants in הָעוֹלָם and God cares about them all. Draw yourself, your family and as many other people, animals and plants as you can on הָעוֹלָם.

The Siddur is printed in Hebrew and in English. This is how an open סִדוּר looks. The Hebrew words are on one page and the English words are on the other. Connect each Hebrew word to the English word that says the same thing.

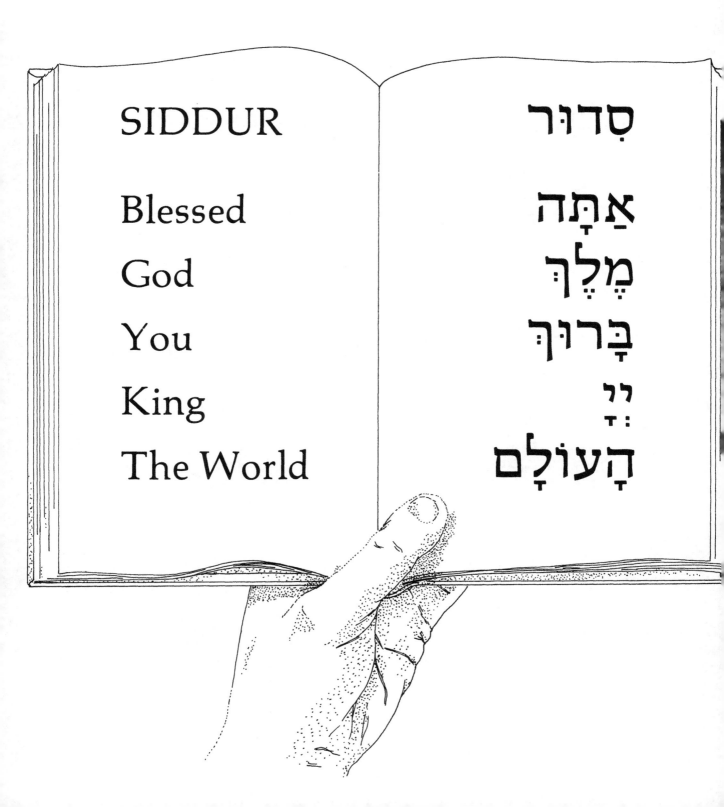

SIDDUR	סִדוּר
Blessed	אַתָּה
God	מֶלֶךְ
You	בָּרוּךְ
King	יְיָ
The World	הָעוֹלָם

You now know the first six words of many, many prayers

בָּרוּךְ אַתָּה יְיָ אֱלֹהֵינוּ מֶלֶךְ הָעוֹלָם

"Blessed are You, Adonai, our God, ruler of the world"

The words always go in this order, just like the letters of your name.

Write your name here _____

Now write the letters of your name in a different order _____

Would you like to be called that? It would sound funny. We get used to pronouncing your name in one way, so that is what we say when you mean YOU! Our prayers always have words in the right order. That's the Jewish way. Cut out the six Hebrew words and paste them on the spaces in the correct order.

מֶלֶךְ	יְיָ	בָּרוּךְ
אֱלֹהֵינוּ	אַתָּה	הָעוֹלָם

Whenever a prayer starts with these six words

בָּרוּךְ אַתָּה יְיָ אֱלֹהֵינוּ מֶלֶךְ הָעוֹלָם

we call the prayer a blessing — בְּרָכָה. When we say a blessing, we say "thank you" to God. We have all kinds of blessings.

We say a בְּרָכָה before we eat.

We say a בְּרָכָה when we light candles.

We even have a בְּרָכָה to say when we see a rainbow. Draw a picture showing how you would look saying a blessing when you see a rainbow.

How many blessings can you find on this Siddur page? Remember, every time you see the six words בְּרָכָה a, בָּרוּךְ אַתָּה יְיָ אֱלֹהֵינוּ מֶלֶךְ הָעוֹלָם has begun.

בָּרוּךְ אַתָּה יְיָ אֱלֹהֵינוּ מֶלֶךְ הָעוֹלָם
אֲשֶׁר קִדְּשָׁנוּ בְּמִצְוֹתָיו וְצִוָּנוּ
לְהַדְלִיק נֵר שֶׁל שַׁבָּת.

בָּרוּךְ אַתָּה יְיָ אֱלֹהֵינוּ מֶלֶךְ הָעוֹלָם
בּוֹרֵא פְּרִי הַגָּפֶן.

בָּרוּךְ אַתָּה יְיָ אֱלֹהֵינוּ מֶלֶךְ הָעוֹלָם
הַמּוֹצִיא לֶחֶם מִן הָאָרֶץ.

בָּרוּךְ אַתָּה יְיָ אֱלֹהֵינוּ מֶלֶךְ הָעוֹלָם
שֶׁהֶחֱיָנוּ וְקִיְּמָנוּ וְהִגִּיעָנוּ לַזְּמַן הַזֶּה.

Every time we hear the words בָּרוּךְ אַתָּה or see the words in the Siddur, a בְּרָכָה has begun. When the בְּרָכָה is over, we say Amen — אָמֵן. Like a train, בָּרוּךְ אַתָּה is the engine at the beginning and אָמֵן is the caboose at the end. Fill in אָמֵן at the end of each בְּרָכָה.

Near the beginning of our synagogue service, the leader gives us a signal to show it is time for us to praise God together. The signal is a word — בָּרְכוּ. When the leader says בָּרְכוּ, we all stand and we all praise God together. Color the spaces with dots with the same crayon to see the בָּרְכוּ signal. Then color the rest of the spaces with different crayons to make a stained glass window.

בָּרְכוּ אֶת ־ יְיָ הַמְבֹרָךְ.
בָּרוּךְ יְיָ הַמְבֹרָךְ לְעוֹלָם וָעֶד.

A very important prayer in our סִדּוּר is called שְׁמַע. שְׁמַע means "Hear!" It means we must "listen." In the שְׁמַע, God is talking to us. Look closely at the picture and see if you can find the name of the prayer.

You have several names. You have a first name and a last name. You probably have a middle name too. You have an English name and a Hebrew name.

One of the names we Jews call ourselves is Israel. This is the way Israel looks in Hebrew — יִשְׂרָאֵל. No matter where Jews live in the world, we all call ourselves יִשְׂרָאֵל. So now you know another one of your names. You too are called יִשְׂרָאֵל. Here are some members of our Jewish family, the family of Israel.

In the שְׁמַע God tells us an important thing we should know: GOD IS ONE. The Hebrew word for one is אֶחָד. Connect the numbers to see the Hebrew word and its meaning.

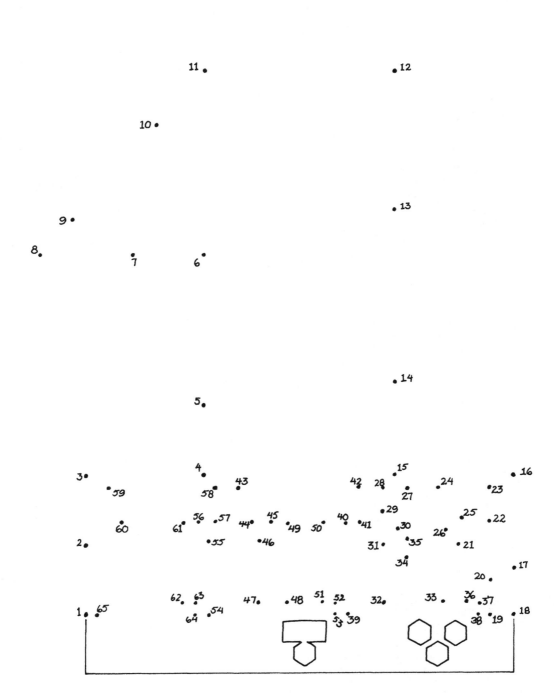

Do you know the meaning of the Hebrew words in the שְׁמַע? Connect each Hebrew word in the Siddur to the English word that says the same thing.

SIDDUR

Hear

Israel

Our God

One

God

סִדּוּר

יְיָ

שְׁמַע

אֱלֹהֵינוּ

יִשְׂרָאֵל

אֶחָד

You know the meanings of the words in the **שְׁמַע**.
The words of the **שְׁמַע** are so important, we learn them by heart. We say them at night before we go to sleep. Color the words in the **שְׁמַע** to see them more clearly. Then learn the words by heart so you can say them every night before you go to sleep.

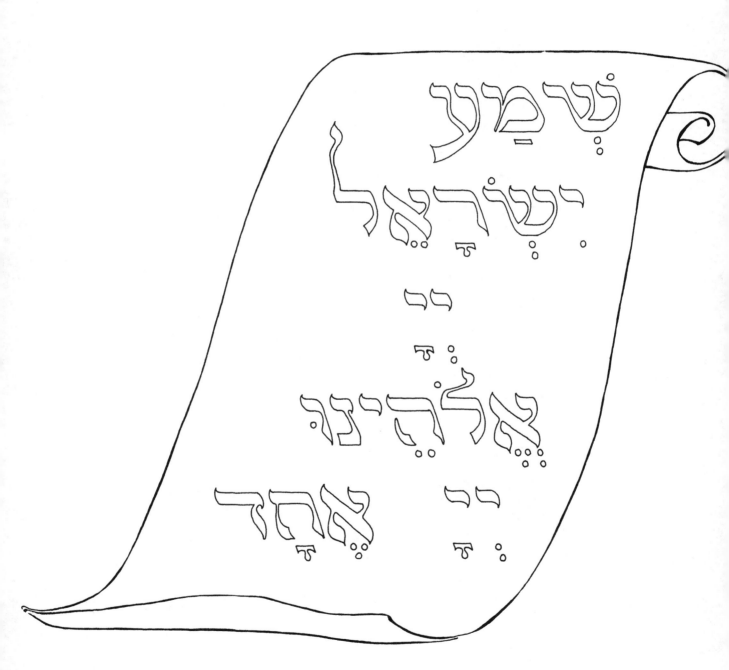

We ask God for many things. We pray to יְיָ and ask for health. We pray for peace. And we are thankful for all the good things we have. But what can we do for יְיָ? In the שְׁמַע God tells us what we must do. The שְׁמַע tells us to love God. The word we use is וְאָהַבְתָּ. It means, "you shall love." Color the pictures that tell us how we can show that we love God.

וְאָהַבְתָּ אֵת יְיָ אֱלֹהֶיךָ.

Many of our prayers praise God. Many thank יְיָ for all the wonderful things in our lives. And sometimes we ask יְיָ for things. We ask for ourselves and for our family, and for all the people in the world. The part of the synagogue service when we ask is called the Amidah - עֲמִידָה. עֲמִידָה means standing. We stand quietly and think about the important things we need. Draw a picture of something you want to ask God for.

During the עֲמִידָה we say an important prayer. It is called Kedushah. The word
Kedushah comes from the Hebrew word *kadosh* - קָדוֹשׁ. קָדוֹשׁ means different and
special and holy. We all sing about God's holiness. We all sing קָדוֹשׁ קָדוֹשׁ קָדוֹשׁ.
Color the spaces with dots with the same crayon to see the three Hebrew words. Then
color the rest of the spaces with different crayons to make a stained glass window.

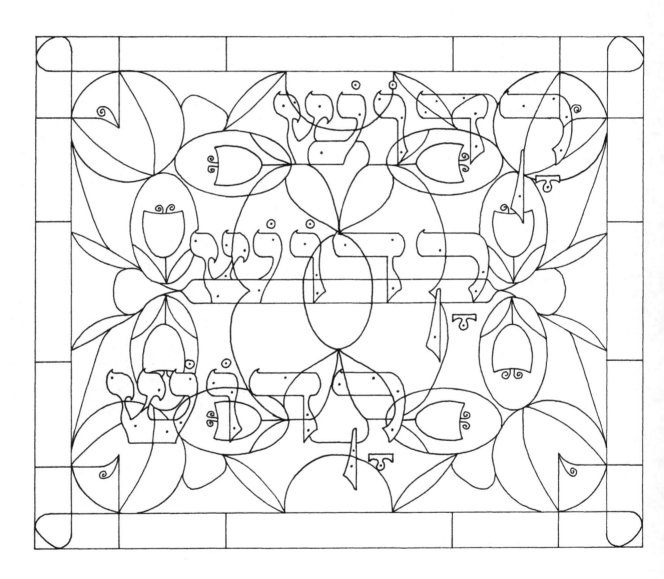

קָדוֹשׁ. קָדוֹשׁ. קָדוֹשׁ. יְיָ צְבָאוֹת.

One of the things we ask God for in the עֲמִידָה is peace. The Hebrew word for peace is שָׁלוֹם. When we have שָׁלוֹם, many other good things are carried into our lives. Paste the pictures on the basket to help carry שָׁלוֹם into your life.

עוֹשֶׂה שָׁלוֹם בִּמְרוֹמָיו
הוּא יַעֲשֶׂה שָׁלוֹם.

During the **עֲמִידָה**, we remember that God helped the first Jewish people who lived long, long ago. Three of them were especially close to **יְיָ**. Their names were Abraham — **אַבְרָהָם**, Isaac — **יִצְחָק**, and Jacob — **יַעֲקֹב**. The picture shows what God promised to **אַבְרָהָם, יִצְחָק**, and **יַעֲקֹב**. Color the map.

Can you learn the names of the 5 cities on the map?

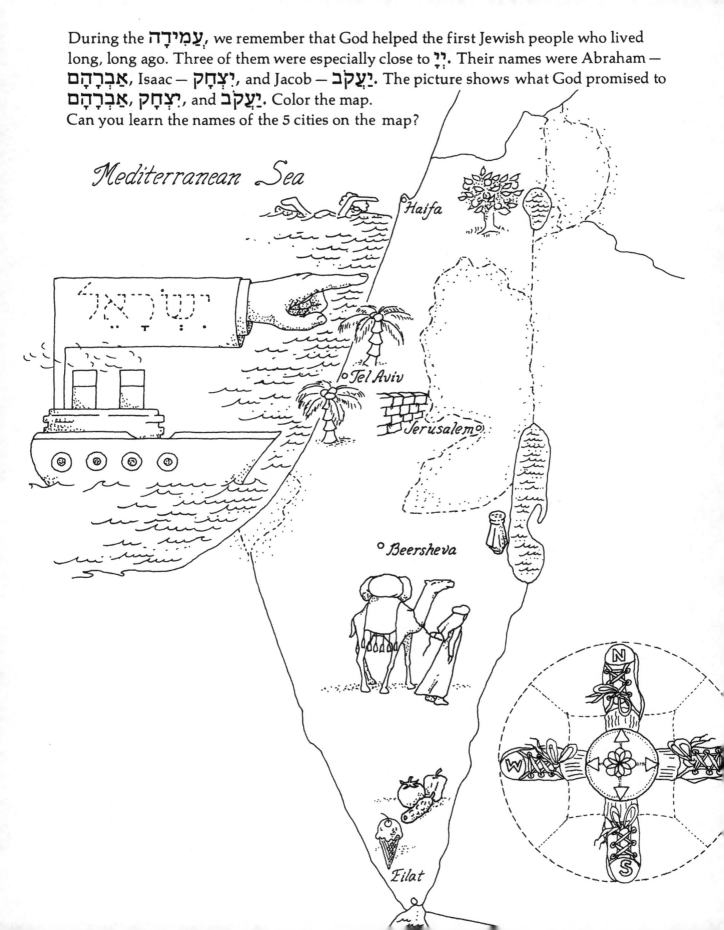

Mediterranean Sea

יְיָ

Haifa

Tel Aviv

Jerusalem

Beersheva

Eilat

N

W

S

One of the last תְּפִלּוֹת we say in the synagogue is called עָלֵינוּ.

עָלֵינוּ לְשַׁבֵּחַ לַאֲדוֹן הַכֹּל

The עָלֵינוּ prayer says that we Jews are different from other people. We have special things to do. Each picture shows something that Jewish people do.
Can you recognize each thing that makes us special?

During the synagogue service, people remember members of their family who have died. Sometimes people feel very sad when they remember because they miss the person so much. They stand and say the mourner's prayer called Kaddish — קָדִישׁ. When they finish the קָדִישׁ prayer, the congregation says אָמֵן. Complete the words and then color the picture.

יִתְגַּדַל וְיִתְקַדַשׁ שְׁמֵהּ רַבָּא.

One of our favorite prayers comes at the end of the synagogue service. It is called אֵין כֵּאלֹהֵינוּ. It means, "There is nothing like our God!" Cut out and match the puzzle pieces to see that אֵין כֵּאלֹהֵינוּ !

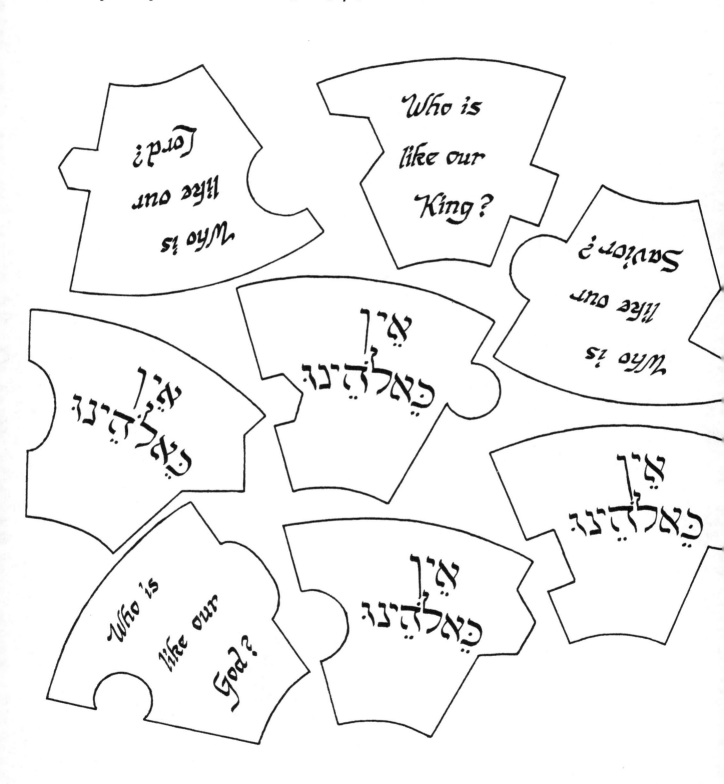

When we say our **תְּפִלּוֹת**, we try our best to pronounce the words just right. We sing the songs in our best voices. The more we practice, the easier it is to do. We also try to think about what we are saying, and we try to mean what we say. That is very hard to do and it doesn't always get easier. But when we do it — when we really think about our prayers and we really mean what we say, then we have **כַּוָּנָה**. Find your way up the ladder to reach **כַּוָּנָה**.

On the next four pages there are word cards to cut out. You can use the cards to practice the prayers words you have learned. You can put them together in the right order to make prayers. And you can combine them with someone else's set to play a matching game.

תְּפִלּוֹת	סִדּוּר
יְיָ	בָּרוּךְ
אַתָּה	אֱלֹהֵינוּ
מֶלֶךְ	הָעוֹלָם

בְּרָכָה	בָּרְכוּ
שְׁמַע	יִשְׂרָאֵל
יְיָ	אֱלֹהֵינוּ
יְיָ	אֶחָד

עֲמִידָה	וְאָהַבְתָּ
קָדוֹשׁ	קָדוֹשׁ
שָׁלוֹם	קָדוֹשׁ
יִצְחָק	אַבְרָהָם

יַעֲקֹב	עָלֵינוּ
קַדִישׁ	אָמֵן
אֵין	כֵּאלֹהֵינוּ
כַּוָּנָה	אָמֵן